TX
809
.M17
M347
2000
HWLCTC

BUSINESS/SCIENCE/TECHNOLOGY DIVISION
CHICAGO PUBLIC LIBRARY
400 SOUTH STATE STREET
CHICAGO, IL 60605

Chicago Public Library

W9-APD-573

Recipes from the vineyards of North

RECIPES

from the

VINEYARDS

of

NORTHERN
CALIFORNIA

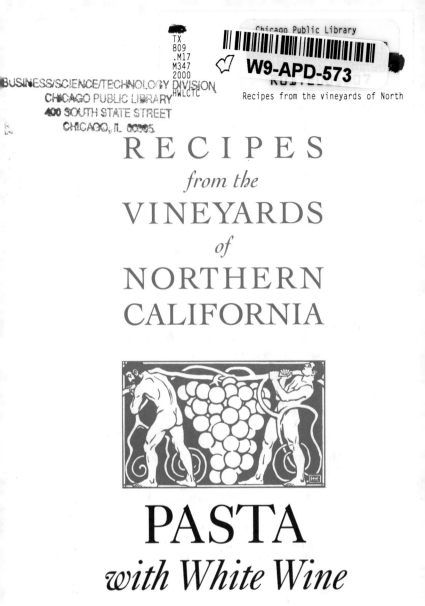

PASTA

with White Wine

Leslie Mansfield

CELESTIALARTS

Berkeley, California

When preparing recipes that call for egg yolks or whites, whether or not they are to be cooked, use only the highest quality, salmonella-free eggs.

Copyright © 2000 by Leslie Mansfield

All rights reserved. No part of this book may be reproduced in any form, except brief excerpts for the purpose of review, without the written permission of the publisher.

CELESTIALARTS
P.O. Box 7123
Berkeley, California 94707

Distributed in Canada by Ten Speed Canada, in the United Kingdom and Europe by Airlift Books, in New Zealand by Southern Publishers Group, in Australia by Simon & Schuster Australia, in South Africa by Real Books, and in Singapore, Malaysia, Hong Kong, and Thailand by Berkeley Books.

Cover and interior design by Greene Design
Cover photograph by Larry Kunkel
Photo styling by Veronica Randall
Public Domain Art thanks to Dover Publications

Library of Congress Card Catalog Number 99-80107

First printing, 2000
Printed in the United States

1 2 3 4 5 6 7 — 03 02 01 00

BST
OPN

BUSINESS/SCIENCE/TECHNOLOGY DIVISION
CHICAGO PUBLIC LIBRARY
400 SOUTH STATE STREET
CHICAGO, IL 60605

RD172001007

To my mother,

MARCIA WHIPPLE,

whose love of life has been a constant

inspiration.

ACKNOWLEDGMENTS

Deepest gratitude goes to my husband, Richard, who has helped me with every step—his name belongs on the title page along with mine. To my wonderful parents, Stewart and Marcia Whipple for their unflagging confidence. To Phil Wood, who makes dreams a reality. To my dear friend and editor Veronica Randall, whose creativity, intelligence, and wit makes working with Celestial Arts a joy. To Victoria Randall, for her invaluable assistance. To Brad Greene, for another spectacular design. To Larry Kunkel, for his glorious photography.

Finally, this book would not have been possible without the cooperation of all our friends at the wineries who graciously contributed their favorite recipes. I wish to thank them all for their generosity.

Table of Contents

Introduction

🍇 Just mention California wine country and thoughts of warm sunshine, vines heavy with ripening grapes, and a relaxed lifestyle come to mind. The small villages throughout the wine country each have their own personalities, as do the wineries. From rural, family-run boutique wineries to large, stately wineries surrounded by a sea of vineyards, they all have one thing in common, a love for good food and wine.

This love of food and wine has resulted in an explosion of cutting-edge ideas that have defined California cuisine, incorporating the finest of Europe and Asia, while drawing on the incredible local and seasonal bounty.

Entertaining is a way of life in wine country. Whether it is a formal dinner with many courses to showcase a variety of wines, or just drawing off a pitcher of new wine from the barrel to go with an impromptu picnic with neighbors, the desire to share the best they have to offer has helped shape the cuisine of California.

In the following pages you will find recipes offered from the finest wineries of Northern California. Each reflects the personality of a winery, whether formal or casual, and all are delicious. Each one is a taste of wine country.

ARROWOOD VINEYARDS AND WINERY

Richard Arrowood, one of California's most renowned winemakers, along with his wife and partner Alis Demers Arrowood, have crafted a winery that sits in perfect harmony with its environs. Fashioned after a New England farmhouse, the winery has often been described as a "winemaker's dream." Maker of a number of wonderful, rare, and outstanding wines, Richard Arrowood uses his intimate knowledge of the Sonoma Valley's many microclimates and terroirs *to create great and complex wines.*

PASTA
with Swiss Chard & Anchovies

The anchovies give a subliminal lift to this sublimely delicate summer dish.

1/4 cup olive oil, divided

1 onion, finely chopped

1 pound Swiss chard, chopped

1/4 cup Arrowood Vineyards and Winery Viognier

1 tablespoon minced anchovies

1/4 teaspoon dried hot chile flakes

Salt and freshly ground black pepper to taste

1 pound fusilli pasta, cooked in boiling salted water
    until al dente, then drained

In a large skillet, heat 3 tablespoons of the olive oil over medium heat. Add onion and sauté until tender. Add Swiss chard and sauté just until wilted. Add wine, anchovies, and chile flakes and simmer for 5 minutes. Stir in remaining olive oil. Season with salt and pepper. Gently stir in pasta and toss to coat well.

Serves 6
*Serve with Arrowood Vineyards
and Winery Viognier*

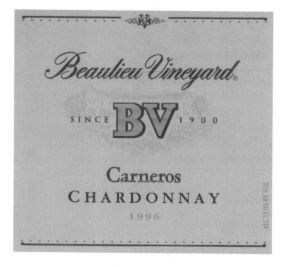

BEAULIEU VINEYARD

Beaulieu Vineyard (BV) was founded in 1900 by Georges de Latour, who came from a winegrowing family in Bordeaux. Since its inception, BV has been an historic, important player in the history of California winemaking. Under the guidance of legendary winemaker Andre Techelistcheff, beginning in 1938, BV's famous Georges de Latour Cabernet Sauvignon Private Reserve set the standard for California Cabernet through the rest of the century. Madame de Latour, who ran the company in the 1940s was a brilliant and outspoken promoter of BV who even had the audacity to show her family's wines in her native France, and won them over. BV has been a major pioneer of the cool Carneros District of Napa, now legendary for fine Pinot Noir and Chardonnay. The winery is now owned by United Distillers & Vintners North America, and the current winemaker, Joel Aiken, continues the great tradition, along with a fine sense of innovation, established by Georges de Latour and Andre Techelistcheff.

FETTUCCINE
with Sautéed Rock Shrimp & Sundried Tomatoes with Saffron Cream

The delightful flavors are echoed in the beautiful yellows, pinks, reds, and oranges of this dish.

SAFFRON CREAM:

1 tablespoon olive oil

2 shallots, minced

1 cup Beaulieu Vineyard Chardonnay

1 teaspoon saffron threads

1 bay leaf

1 cup chicken stock

2 cups heavy cream

Salt and freshly ground black pepper to taste

3 tablespoons olive oil

12 ounces rock shrimp

Salt and freshly ground black pepper to taste

2 tablespoons chopped garlic

1/4 cup Beaulieu Vineyard Chardonnay

1/2 cup thinly sliced sundried tomatoes

1/4 cup lightly packed fresh basil leaves, thinly sliced

1 pound fettuccine, cooked in boiling salted water until al dente, then drained

Freshly grated Parmesan cheese

(recipe continued on next page)

For the saffron cream: In a saucepan, heat the olive oil over medium heat. Add the shallots and sauté until tender. Stir in the wine, saffron, and bay leaf and simmer until liquid is reduced to 1/4 cup. Stir in the chicken stock and simmer until the liquid is reduced to 1/2 cup. Stir in the cream and simmer until the liquid is reduced by half. Season with salt and pepper. Strain through a fine sieve and discard the solids. Set aside.

In a skillet, heat olive oil over medium-high heat. Season the shrimp with salt and pepper and add to skillet. Sauté just until shrimp turns pink. Remove with a slotted spoon and set aside. Add the garlic and sauté until fragrant. Whisk in the wine, scraping up any browned bits. Stir in the reserved saffron cream sauce and reduce heat to medium. Simmer until mixture is reduced by one third. Stir in sundried tomatoes and basil. Stir in hot pasta and shrimp and simmer until heated through. Divide onto 6 plates and sprinkle with Parmesan. Serve immediately.

Serves 6
Serve with Beaulieu Vineyard
Chardonnay

BENZIGER FAMILY WINERY

The Benziger Family, producers of Benziger Family, Reserve, and Imagery Wines, believes that the nature of great wine lies in vineyard character, winemaker artistry, and family passion. At Benziger this means farming and vinifying select vineyards to mine the unique character of each, winemaking that combines intuition and artistry with a minimalist philosophy, and passion that is shared by the entire family. In its quest for uniqueness through diversity, each year the family produces over 300 lots of grapes from over sixty ranches in over a dozen appellations.

SAUTÉED ABALONE & PASTA

Genie Mosey, chef at the Benziger Family Winery, developed this wonderful dish to showcase the beautiful combination of abalone and their Fumé Blanc.

2 tablespoons olive oil, divided

1 onion, chopped

1 teaspoon minced garlic

$1^{1}/2$ cups chicken stock

8 ounces Roma tomatoes, seeded and chopped

Salt and freshly ground black pepper to taste

1 tablespoon butter

12 ounces abalone, thoroughly pounded until tenderized and sliced into $3/4$-inch strips

12 ounces somen noodles or vermicelli, cooked in boiling salted water until al dente, then drained

$1/2$ cup snipped fresh chives

In a saucepan, heat 1 tablespoon of the olive oil over medium heat. Add the onion and garlic and sauté until tender. Add chicken stock and simmer until mixture is reduced by half. Add tomatoes and simmer until heated through. Season with salt and pepper and set aside.

In a skillet, heat the remaining olive oil and butter over medium-high heat. Season the abalone with salt and pepper and add to the sizzling oil mixture. Stir-fry for about 1 to 3 minutes, or until just cooked through. Do not overcook or the abalone will become tough.

To serve, toss tomato mixture with hot pasta. Divide pasta onto 4 plates and top with abalone. Sprinkle with chives and serve immediately.

Serves 4
Serve with Benziger Family Winery
Fumé Blanc

BELVEDERE VINEYARDS AND WINERY

In Italian, "belvedere" means "beautiful view," which aptly describes the vista from this rustic redwood winery in the Russian River Valley. The winery was built in 1982, which was the same year owners Bill and Sally Hambrecht bought their first piece of vineyard land high atop Bradford Mountain in Dry Creek Valley. Over the years they purchased and planted additional estate vineyards in the Dry Creek, Alexander, and Russian River Valleys in Northern Sonoma County. As Bill Hambrecht often says, "Our most valuable asset is our vineyards. Good vineyards are as valuable as gold to a winery, and Belvedere has access to some of Sonoma County's best."

RABBIT STEW
with Chanterelles &
Saffron over Fettuccine

*Serve this hearty main course to your
favorite "vintner" after a day of work in
your winter garden.*

1 rabbit, cut into serving pieces

Salt and freshly ground black pepper to taste

Flour for dredging

3 tablespoons olive oil

1 teaspoon sugar

1 onion, chopped

6 cloves garlic, minced

1 1/2 cups Belvedere Vineyards and Winery
  Chardonnay

1/2 cup chicken stock

1/2 teaspoon saffron threads

1/8 teaspoon cayenne

2 tablespoons butter

8 ounces chanterelles, thickly sliced

1 pound fettuccine

2 tablespoons minced fresh tarragon

(recipe continued on next page)

❧ Season the rabbit with salt and pepper. Dredge lightly in flour and shake off excess. In a skillet large enough to hold the rabbit in a single layer, heat olive oil over medium-high heat. Add the rabbit pieces and lightly brown on all sides. Sprinkle the rabbit with sugar and continue to cook until well browned. Remove the rabbit to a plate and set aside.

Add the onion and garlic to the skillet and sauté until just tender. Whisk in wine, chicken stock, saffron, and cayenne, scraping up any browned bits. Return rabbit to the skillet, along with any accumulated juices, and bring to a boil. Reduce heat to medium-low, cover, and simmer for about 1 hour, or until rabbit is very tender. When rabbit is done, remove to a plate and keep warm. If the sauce is too thin, simmer uncovered to reduce and thicken.

In a separate skillet, heat the butter over medium heat. Add the chanterelles and sauté until tender. Set aside.

Bring a large pot of salted water to a boil. Stir in the fettuccine and cook until al dente, then drain. Add the pasta to the sauce in the skillet and stir gently until it is thoroughly coated and sauce is thick. Put fettuccine in a large shallow pasta bowl and nestle rabbit pieces in the pasta. Top with chanterelles and sprinkle with tarragon.

Serves 6 to 8
Serve with Belvedere Vineyards and Winery
Chardonnay

Good wine is a good familiar creature if it be well used.

Shakespeare

BERINGER VINEYARDS

The oldest continually operating winery in the Napa Valley was started in 1876 by Jacob and Frederick Beringer, immigrants from Mainz, Germany. Currently a publicly traded company, owned by thousands of wine-loving shareholders, Beringer Vineyards excels in the production of vineyard designated reds, graceful and supple whites, and lovingly tended, botrytis-affected, late harvest dessert wines.

MASCARPONE & ROASTED GARLIC RAVIOLI *with* Tomato Jus & Basil Oil

This imaginative first course from Beringer Vineyards' executive chef, Jerry Comfort, can also double as a main entrée for an intimate dinner.

BASIL OIL:

1 bunch basil

1/2 cup olive oil

TOMATO JUS:

3 cups Beringer Vineyards Chardonnay

6 large ripe tomatoes, quartered

1 1/2 tablespoons freshly squeezed lemon juice

Salt and white pepper to taste

MASCARPONE AND ROASTED GARLIC RAVIOLI:

1 head garlic

1 tablespoon olive oil

8 ounces mascarpone cheese

Salt and freshly ground black pepper to taste

1 egg

1 tablespoon water

36 round wonton skins

6 sprigs basil for garnish

(recipe continued on next page)

For the basil oil: Trim the leaves from the basil and discard the stems. Blanch the basil in boiling salted water for 10 seconds, drain, and then plunge into a bowl of ice water. Drain well. Purée in a blender or food processor, then transfer to a bowl. Gently stir in the olive oil. Let the mixture infuse overnight, stirring occasionally. The next day, ladle off the brilliant green oil, and discard the solids. Pour into a clean jar and cover. Store in the refrigerator.

For the tomato jus: In a saucepan, simmer wine over medium heat until liquid is reduced to $3/4$ cup. Set aside.

Put tomatoes in the bowl of a food processor and process until smooth. Place tomato purée in a saucepan and simmer over medium-low heat for 30 minutes. Strain through a fine sieve and discard the solids. Return tomato liquid to a saucepan and stir in reserved wine and lemon juice. Season to taste with salt and white pepper. Set aside. Bring to a simmer right before serving.

For the ravioli: Preheat oven to 400°F.

Remove the papery outer skins from the garlic, leaving the whole head intact. Slice $1/4$-inch off the top. Set in the middle of a piece of foil and drizzle with olive oil. Bake for about 1 hour or until garlic is very tender. Remove from oven and cool.

Squeeze garlic out of skins. Place roasted garlic and mascarpone in the bowl of a food processor and pulse until smooth. Season with salt and pepper. In a small bowl, whisk together egg and water to make an egg wash.

Place a wonton skin on a work surface and brush lightly with egg wash. Place a tablespoon of filling in the center. Place another wonton skin on top and seal the edges together. Lightly sprinkle a baking sheet with flour. Place ravioli on baking sheet so that they are not touching each other. Continue until all filling is used.

Bring a large pot of salted water to a boil. Add the ravioli and cook until they rise to the surface, about 4 minutes. Drain and divide ravioli into 6 shallow bowls. Ladle hot tomato jus over and drizzle with basil oil. Garnish with a sprig of basil.

Serves 6
Serve with Beringer Vineyards
Chardonnay

Cakebread Cellars

NAPA VALLEY

Sauvignon Blanc

1997

ALCOHOL 13.5% BY VOLUME

CAKEBREAD CELLARS

A *true family winery, Cakebread Cellars in Rutherford is one of the most creative and successful wineries in California's famed Napa Valley. Since its founding in 1973, the winery has developed a reputation for producing world-class wines and pairing them with outstanding cuisine. Dolores Cakebread, the winery's culinary director, had the vision to plant vegetable gardens at the same time their vineyards were being planted. She has been a forerunner in the development of "California cuisine," which emphasizes fresh, natural, and locally grown produce to complement the wines of Cakebread Cellars.*

RISOTTO
with Crab, Sweet Corn, & Green Chiles

Although the origins of risotto lie in Northern Italy, Cakebread's version clearly shows its West Coast influence.

1 Anaheim chile

3 tablespoons olive oil, divided

1/2 cup finely chopped onion

2 cloves garlic, minced

1 cup arborio rice

5 cups chicken stock

1 cup fresh corn kernels

4 ounces crab meat, picked over

2 tablespoons freshly grated Parmesan cheese

1 tablespoon Cakebread Cellars Chardonnay

Salt and freshly ground black pepper to taste

❧ Preheat oven to 450°F.

Place chile on a baking sheet and sprinkle with 1 tablespoon of olive oil. Roast in the oven for about 20 minutes, or until blackened all over. Remove from oven and place hot chile in a plastic bag. Set aside to steam in the bag until cool.

(recipe continued on next page)

Peel off the skin and discard. Cut the chile into a fine dice and set aside.

In a large saucepan, heat the remaining 2 tablespoons olive oil over medium heat. Add onion and garlic and sauté until tender. Add the rice and toss to coat. In a saucepan, bring the chicken stock to a simmer over medium-low heat. Ladle enough simmering stock into the rice to just cover the rice. Lower the heat under the rice to medium-low and stir constantly until almost all of the liquid has been absorbed. Add more simmering stock to just cover the rice and continue stirring until almost absorbed. Repeat this process until the rice is tender but still firm. This will take about 20 minutes. After the first 10 minutes, stir in the corn and reserved chile. When almost done, stir in the crab, Parmesan, and wine and season with salt and pepper. Serve immediately.

Serves 2 as a main course or 4 as a side dish.
Serve with Cakebread Cellars
Chardonnay

CANYON ROAD WINERY

One of Sonoma County's more picturesque settings, Canyon Road Winery is a favorite among wine country visitors. A warm and friendly tasting room features award winning Canyon Road wines, including some limited selections available only at the winery. Enjoy a country deli and gift shop, picnic areas by the vines, complimentary wine tasting, and always great hospitality.

PASTA SALAD *with* *Cherry Tomatoes, Arugula, & Kalamata Olives*

Pull this summer salad out of your next picnic hamper and you'll enjoy an unforgettable summer experience.

3 tablespoons white wine vinegar

1 teaspoon salt

$1/2$ teaspoon freshly ground black pepper

$1/3$ cup olive oil

10 ounces cherry tomatoes, quartered

6 ounces arugula, chopped

$1/3$ cup finely chopped Kalamata olives

12 ounces farfalle (bowtie) pasta

In a large serving bowl, whisk together vinegar, salt, and pepper until salt dissolves. Whisk in olive oil. Add tomatoes, arugula, and olives and toss to coat with dressing.

Cook pasta in boiling salted water until al dente, then drain. Let pasta cool slightly then add to bowl and toss gently to coat with dressing and distribute vegetables. Taste and add more salt and pepper if necessary.

Serves 6
Serve with Canyon Road Winery
Sauvignon Blanc

Wine comes in at the mouth
And love comes in at the eye;
That's all we shall know for truth
Before we grow old and die.

Yeats

CARDINALE WINERY

Cardinale Rule: Make grape selection an obsession and gentle winemaking a virtue. Grow fruit of intense vineyard and varietal character from the finest sites in the Mayacamas. Pick only when the fruit is physiologically ripe and balanced in flavor. Hand harvest into small lug boxes, during the cool of the morning. Keep each vineyard separate, in order to know it better. Hand sort all fruit and use only sound, ripe berries. Carefully crack the berries and begin native yeast fermentation. Gently macerate juice and skins for 25 to 35 days to maximize flavor and texture. Use a traditional basket press to deepen mid-palate flavors. Place into 100% new, tight-grained French oak Chateau barrels. Attentively rack wine from barrel to barrel every three months. Age in barrel for 18 to 21 months. Bottle unfiltered. Age in bottle for 12 months before release. Enjoy or bottle age for an additional 5 to 10 years.

SPAGHETTI *with* Gorgonzola & Walnuts

Serve this savory spaghetti dish with a green salad for a light supper.

2 tablespoons butter

2 cloves garlic, crushed

4 ounces Gorgonzola, crumbled

1/4 cup sour cream

3/4 cup finely chopped walnuts

Salt and freshly ground white pepper to taste

12 ounces spaghetti, cooked in boiling salted water until al dente, then drained

In a large saucepan, melt butter over medium heat. Add garlic and sauté until fragrant. Add the crumbled Gorgonzola and stir until melted. Add sour cream and stir to make a creamy sauce. Stir in the walnuts. Season with salt and pepper. Add the spaghetti to the sauce in the pan, stir gently until coated, and serve immediately.

Serves 4
Serve with Cardinale Winery
Royale Meritage

CEDAR MOUNTAIN
WINERY

*The creative interests of Linda and Earl Ault
came to fruition in 1990 when they established
Cedar Mountain Winery and began production of their award winning wines. True to
their belief that quality wines begin with the
finest grapes in the vineyard, the Aults special-
ize in wines from fruit grown locally in the
Livermore Valley. In addition to the classic
Chardonnays and Bordelais varieties from
these vineyards, a small amount of Port grown
in the Sierra Foothills is also produced.*

LINGUINE
with Morels & Asparagus

*This delicate pasta dish from Sigrid Laing
would be excellent served to celebrate the first
warm day of spring.*

2 cups Cedar Mountain Winery Chardonnay

1 ounce dried morel mushrooms

3 tablespoons olive oil

2 tablespoons minced shallots

12 ounces asparagus, cut into 1-inch pieces

1 cup heavy cream

1 tablespoon butter, softened

1 tablespoon all-purpose flour

2 tablespoons chopped chives

1 teaspoon minced fresh thyme

1 teaspoon salt

9 ounces fresh linguine

1/2 cup freshly grated Parmesan cheese

2 tablespoons pine nuts, lightly toasted

(recipe continued on next page)

In a small saucepan, heat the wine until almost boiling. Remove from heat and add the morels. Let stand 45 minutes to soften. With a slotted spoon, remove morels and chop. Reserve liquid.

In a saucepan, heat olive oil over medium heat. Add shallots and sauté until tender. Add morels and sauté until golden brown. Add reserved liquid and simmer until liquid is reduced by half. Add asparagus and simmer until just tender. Stir in cream.

In a small bowl, blend butter and flour together until smooth. Whisk in $1/4$ cup of the hot liquid to the flour mixture until smooth. Pour mixture back into the saucepan and stir until blended. Simmer over medium-low heat, stirring constantly, until slightly thickened. Stir in chives, thyme, and salt.

Cook linguine in boiling salted water until al dente. Drain well, then add to the sauce. Stir gently and simmer until heated through and pasta is well coated. Serve in a large shallow bowl. Sprinkle with Parmesan and pine nuts.

Serves 4
Serve with Cedar Mountain Winery
Chardonnay

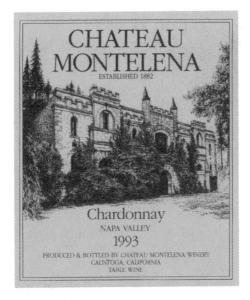

CHATEAU MONTELENA WINERY

A visit to Chateau Montelena is a must for wine lovers seeking excellence. With thick natural stone walls, which maintain perfect temperature and humidity for aging wine, and the exceptional grapes that come from their Estate Vineyard, Chateau Montelena has earned its reputation as one of California's first growths. Even the French, for the first time in the history of winemaking, named the Chateau Montelena Winery Chardonnay the world's greatest Chardonnay in 1976.

LINGUINE
with Chicken & Pesto

*Gerard Zanzonico developed this tasty
dish to showcase the Chateau Montelena
Winery Chardonnay.*

1 pound asparagus, cut into 1-inch pieces

1 bunch fresh basil leaves

1/2 cup pine nuts

1/4 cup plus 1 tablespoon olive oil, divided

5 cloves garlic

4 skinless boneless chicken breasts, cut into
    1-inch cubes

Salt and freshly ground black pepper to taste

1 teaspoon dried basil

1/2 cup freshly grated Parmesan cheese

12 ounces linguine, cooked in boiling salted
    water until al dente, then drained

1/2 cup oil-packed sundried tomatoes, drained
    and finely chopped

Steam asparagus until just tender. Set aside.

In the bowl of a food processor, combine fresh basil, pine nuts, 1/4 cup olive oil, and garlic and pulse until smooth. Set aside.

In a skillet, heat remaining 1 tablespoon olive oil over medium heat. Season chicken with salt and pepper. Add chicken to the skillet and sauté until cooked through. Stir in reserved asparagus, reserved basil mixture, dried basil, and Parmesan. Reduce heat to medium-low and simmer until heated through. Add hot pasta and stir gently until well coated. Divide onto 4 plates and sprinkle each with 2 tablespoons sundried tomatoes. Serve immediately.

Serves 4
Serve with Chateau Montelena Winery
Chardonnay

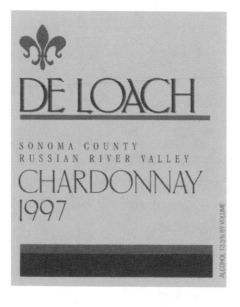

DE LOACH
VINEYARDS

The morning fog along the Russian River Valley, a product of marine influence, is instrumental for the quality of Cecil and Christine De Loach's estate grown wines. This cooling influence in the heat of late summer allows their vines to fully develop their fruit while maintaining acidity and elegance. Cecil and Christine De Loach's personal connection to their vineyards and cellar ensures a consistency of style and excellence in quality year after year.

PENNE *with Pancetta, Peas, & Cream*

This easy-to-make recipe combines Italian bacon and cheeses to produce a heavenly match for the De Loach Sonoma Cuvée Chardonnay.

1^{1}/2 cups heavy cream

3 eggs, lightly beaten

^{2}/3 cup freshly grated Romano cheese

^{1}/3 cup freshly grated Parmesan cheese

^{1}/4 cup olive oil

2 tablespoons butter

2 tablespoons minced garlic

1^{1}/4 pounds pancetta, diced

^{2}/3 cup De Loach Vineyards Sonoma Cuvée
    Chardonnay

1 cup freshly shelled peas

1 pound penne pasta, cooked in boiling salted
    water until al dente, then drained

Salt and freshly ground black pepper to taste

24 snow peas, blanched in boiling water,
    for garnish

(recipe continued on next page)

In a bowl, whisk together cream, eggs, Romano, and Parmesan. Set aside.

In a skillet, heat olive oil and butter over medium heat. Add garlic and sauté until fragrant. Add pancetta and sauté until lightly browned. Whisk in the wine and simmer until the liquid has almost evaporated. Reserve 1/2 cup cooked pancetta for garnish.

Reduce heat to low and whisk cream mixture into the skillet with pancetta. Stir and cook sauce until slightly thickened. Stir in peas and hot pasta. Season with salt and pepper. Simmer until heated through. Divide penne into 8 shallow bowls. Fan 3 snow peas on top and sprinkle with reserved pancetta. Serve immediately.

Serves 8
Serve with De Loach Vineyards Sonoma Cuvée Chardonnay

1992 FUMÉ BLANC
DRY SAUVIGNON BLANC
Sonoma County

DRY CREEK VINEYARD

Dry Creek Vineyard was the first new winery to be established in the Dry Creek Valley of Sonoma after Prohibition. Synonymous with fine winemaking, Dry Creek Vineyard draws upon over 35 different vineyards to produce their wines, matching the particular soils and microclimates of each site to the varieties that do best in the Dry Creek Valley.

PARMESAN-WALNUT CHICKEN *with Mustard Sauce over Fusilli*

Brad Wallace devised this fabulous dish to show off the rich flavors of their Dry Creek Vineyard Fumé Blanc.

4 ounces Parmesan cheese, grated

$1/2$ cup all-purpose flour

$1/3$ cup walnuts

$1/2$ cup milk

4 skinless boneless chicken breasts

Salt and freshly ground black pepper to taste

$1/4$ cup olive oil

1 cup finely chopped onion

$1/2$ cup Dry Creek Vineyard Fumé Blanc

1 cup heavy cream

$1/4$ cup Dijon mustard

12 ounces fusilli pasta, cooked in boiling salted
    water until al dente, then drained

Preheat oven to just warm, about 200°F.

In the bowl of a food processor, combine Parmesan, flour, and walnuts. Pulse until all ingredients are finely ground. Place mixture in a shallow bowl. Place milk in a separate shallow bowl. Lightly pound chicken breasts to a uniform 1/2-inch thickness. Season with salt and pepper. Dredge chicken in Parmesan mixture, pressing to coat well. Dip chicken in milk and dredge again in Parmesan mixture.

In a skillet, heat olive oil over medium-high heat. Add chicken to skillet and cook until golden brown on both sides. Place in oven to keep warm. Add onion to the skillet and sauté until translucent. Whisk in wine and simmer until most of the liquid has evaporated. Whisk in cream and mustard and simmer until slightly thickened. Gently stir hot pasta into sauce until well coated. Divide pasta onto 4 plates and top with warm chicken.

Serves 4
Serve with Dry Creek Vineyard
Fumé Blanc

1996

FERRARI·CARANO

SONOMA COUNTY

Fumé Blanc

SAUVIGNON BLANC
ALCOHOL 13.3% BY VOLUME

FERRARI-CARANO
VINEYARDS AND WINERY

Villa Fiore, or "House of Flowers," at Ferrari-Carano is one of the most spectacular wineries and visitors' centers in the northern California wine country. Designed to reflect the proud Italian heritage of the Carano family, Villa Fiore houses state-of-the-art kitchens, which are used to educate professionals as well as consumers in the enjoyment of Ferrari-Carano wines.

Ferrari-Carano draws its grapes from fourteen winery-owned vineyards over a fifty-mile area from Alexander Valley in the north to the Carneros district in the south. This exceptional supply of fruit allows the winemaker to produce the highly stylized wines for which Ferrari-Carano is known.

FETTUCCINE *with* Scallops & Pesto

An incredibly easy, yet utterly delicious meal.

1 pound asparagus, cut into 2-inch pieces

3 tablespoons butter, divided

2 pounds scallops, quartered

1 (10-ounce) package frozen peas, thawed

3/4 cup heavy cream

2 tablespoons prepared pesto sauce

2 tablespoons freshly squeezed lemon juice

Salt and freshly ground black pepper to taste

1 pound fettuccine, cooked in boiling salted water
   until al dente, then drained

Freshly grated Parmesan cheese

Steam asparagus until barely tender. Set aside.
In a large skillet, melt 2 tablespoons of the butter
over medium heat. Add the scallops and sauté until
barely cooked and still translucent. Add asparagus,
peas, cream, pesto, and lemon juice and simmer
until heated through. Season with salt and pepper.
Add cooked fettuccine and stir gently until pasta is
coated with the sauce. Sprinkle with Parmesan and
serve immediately.

Serves 8
Serve with Ferrari-Carano Winery
Fumé Blanc

GEYSER PEAK WINERY

Located just north of Healdsburg, 100-year-old Geyser Peak Winery's tradition of excellence shows in their being named "1998 Winery of the Year" by Wine & Spirits Magazine *and the San Francisco International Wine Competition. Their original vine covered stone winery is now the cornerstone of a state-of-the-art complex that is one of the most well equipped wineries in California. Within the winery, president and head winemaker, Daryl Groom, oversees the vinification of not only their sought after reserve wines but also a multitude of great wines for all occasions.*

MACARONI &
CHEESE

*If you've never had homemade macaroni and
cheese before, be prepared for a tasty surprise!*

2 tablespoons all-purpose flour

1 teaspoon salt

1/2 teaspoon dry mustard

1/2 teaspoon black pepper

1/4 teaspoon cayenne

3 tablespoons butter, softened

2 1/2 cups milk

2 cups shredded sharp Cheddar cheese

12 ounces macaroni, cooked in boiling salted water
    until al dente, then drained

Preheat oven to 350°F. Lightly oil a 13 x 9-inch
baking dish.

In a large saucepan, stir together flour, salt, mustard, black pepper, and cayenne until well mixed.
Whisk in butter until a smooth paste forms. Cook
over medium-high heat, whisking constantly, for
about 1 minute or until bubbly. Stir in milk and
cook, whisking constantly, until mixture has slightly

(recipe continued on next page)

thickened. Remove from heat and stir in cheese until melted. Stir in hot macaroni and transfer to prepared baking dish. Bake for about 20 minutes, or until the mixture is bubbly and the top begins to turn golden brown.

Serves 8
Serve with Geyser Peak Winery
Chardonnay

Who does not love wine,
women, and song,
Remains a fool his whole life long.

Voss

GLEN ELLEN WINERY

Glen Ellen Winery was created in 1983 by the Benziger family with the idea of producing inexpensive and delicious varietal wines for an increasing number of wine consumers. Thus was born the whole category of "fighting varietals." The winery is located in Sonoma, California, with a wonderful Visitors Center located in the charming town of Glen Ellen in the historic Valley of the Moon, Sonoma County. In 1994, the Benzigers sold the winery to United Distillers & Vintners North America (UDV). UDV continues to produce Glen Ellen Proprietor's Reserve wines with the same degree of dedication to quality; not surprising, as the winemaking team has virtually remained the same for nearly a decade. Glen Ellen utilizes an innovative program, the Grower Feedback Loop, to encourage their many growers to improve the quality of the fruit produced each year to meet consumers' growing sophistication.

WILD MUSHROOM PAPPARDELLE

The only thing that could improve this recipe would be a glass of cool Glen Ellen Winery Chardonnay served alongside.

2 artichokes

Juice of 1 lemon

$1/2$ cup olive oil

1 pound wild mushrooms, such as porcini, chanterelles, or morels, sliced

1 tablespoon minced garlic

2 cups chicken stock

1 tablespoon minced fresh thyme

8 ounces fresh baby spinach

$1/2$ cup lightly packed Italian parsley leaves, minced

4 ounces freshly grated Parmesan cheese, divided

2 tablespoons butter

Salt and freshly ground black pepper to taste

1 pound pappardelle pasta, cooked in boiling salted water until al dente, then drained

Steam the artichokes until just tender. Remove leaves and save for another use. Remove the choke and discard. Slice the artichoke hearts thinly and toss with the lemon juice. Set aside.

In a large skillet, heat olive oil over medium-high heat. Add the mushrooms and sauté until tender. Add the garlic and sauté until fragrant. Stir in the chicken stock and thyme, reduce heat to medium, and simmer until liquid is reduced by half. Stir in the reserved artichoke hearts and simmer until tender. Stir in the spinach and parsley and simmer for 2 minutes. Stir in half of the Parmesan, butter, salt, and pepper. Gently stir in the hot pasta until coated with the sauce. Pour into a large shallow serving bowl and sprinkle remaining Parmesan over the top. Serve immediately.

Serves 6
Serve with Glen Ellen Winery
Chardonnay

GLORIA FERRER
CHAMPAGNE CAVES

Founded by José Ferrer, son of Pedro Ferrer Bosch, the Spanish-Catalan founder of Freixenet, Gloria Ferrer Champagne Caves was opened to the public in July of 1986. Named for José Ferrer's beloved wife, Gloria, Gloria Ferrer has been winning awards and accolades of wine critics ever since. Located in the cool Carneros appellation, Gloria Ferrer's beautiful winery with its stucco walls, arched windows, and overhanging balconies is a piece of the proud history of old Spain.

FETTUCCINE *with*
Shrimp & Fennel
in a Champagne Cream Sauce

Although one doesn't normally require an
excuse to open a bottle of Gloria Ferrer, this
dish will certainly give you one.

3 tablespoons butter

1 pound medium shrimp, peeled and deveined

2 bulbs fennel, thinly sliced

3 shallots, minced

1 cup Gloria Ferrer Champagne Caves Brût

1 tablespoon freshly squeezed lemon juice

1 cup heavy cream

Salt and freshly ground black pepper to taste

1 pound fettuccine, cooked in boiling salted water
until al dente, then drained

Freshly grated Parmesan cheese

In a skillet, heat butter over medium-high heat.
Add shrimp and sauté just until they turn pink.
Remove with a slotted spoon and set aside. Add
fennel and shallots to the skillet and sauté until
fennel is tender. Stir in wine and lemon juice and
simmer until liquid has almost evaporated. Stir in

(recipe continued on next page)

cream and simmer until slightly thickened. Season with salt and pepper. Stir in reserved shrimp along with any accumulated juices. Gently stir hot pasta into sauce to coat well. Divide onto 6 plates and sprinkle with Parmesan.

Serves 6
Serve with Gloria Ferrer Champagne Caves Brût

*A true German can't stand the French,
Yet willingly he drinks their wines.*

Goethe

GRGICH HILLS CELLAR

Grgich Hills Cellar, a collaboration between Miljenko Grgich and Austin Hills of the Hills Bros. Coffee family, has become known as the producer of big, mouth-filling Chardonnays, which connoisseurs consider to be among the finest of the world.

In addition to their incomparable Chardonnays, Grgich Hills produces a lush and firm Cabernet Sauvignon from estate vineyards in Yountville, as well as a delightfully clean and fruity Fumé Blanc from their Olive Hills estate vineyard. Of particular interest are their dry-land farmed Zinfandels, grown on hot and windy hillside vineyard sites. These massive wines have impressive fruit and longevity.

PORK & MUSHROOMS
with Hot Paprika Cream Sauce over Pappardelle

The pleasant warmth of the hot paprika in this hearty autumn dish is readily cooled by the Grgich Hills Cellar Fumé Blanc.

2 tablespoons olive oil

1 pound lean pork, cut into $1/2$-inch cubes

Salt and freshly ground black pepper to taste

1 cup Grgich Hills Cellar Fumé Blanc

1 tablespoon freshly squeezed lemon juice

3 tablespoons butter

1 onion, chopped

1 clove garlic, minced

6 ounces mushrooms, sliced

1 tablespoon hot paprika

1 teaspoon thyme

1 cup heavy cream

$1/2$ cup sour cream

$3/4$ teaspoon salt

1 pound pappardelle, cooked in boiling salted water until al dente, then drained

Minced fresh parsley

In a skillet, heat olive oil over medium-high heat. Season pork cubes with salt and pepper, then add to the skillet and sauté until lightly browned. Stir in wine and lemon juice and simmer until liquid has almost evaporated. Remove from heat and set aside.

In a large saucepan, heat butter over medium heat. Add onion and garlic and sauté until tender. Add mushrooms and sauté until tender. Stir in paprika and thyme and sauté for 1 minute. Stir in cream until blended. Stir in reserved pork and its liquid. Cover, reduce heat to medium-low, and simmer for about 45 minutes, or until pork is very tender. Stir occasionally to prevent scorching. Stir in sour cream and salt and heat through. Serve over pasta and sprinkle with parsley.

Serves 6
Serve with Grgich Hills Cellar
Fumé Blanc

Estate 1994 Grown

HANDLEY

ANDERSON VALLEY CHARDONNAY

HANDLEY CELLARS

Known as much for her exquisite sparkling wines as her superbly crafted still wines, Milla Handley practices her craft at the cellars she and her husband Rex McClellan founded in 1975. Set in the Northwest end of the Anderson Valley, protected to the west by redwood covered coastal ridges and to the east by oak studded hills, Handley Cellars is situated in a unique viticultural region. The Mendocino appellation, by virtue of its cool foggy nights and gentle summers, is ideally suited to the production of aromatic and delicate whites, luscious and elegant reds, and crisp and flavorful sparklers.

FETTUCCINE *with* *Roasted Red Pepper Sauce*

Drive the coastal fog away with this warm and delicious dish featuring the superlative wines of Handley Cellars.

ROASTED PEPPER PURÉE:

3 red bell peppers, cut in half and seeded

1/4 cup olive oil

2 teaspoons freshly squeezed lemon juice

2 tablespoons butter

1 onion, finely chopped

1/2 cup Handley Cellars Dry Creek Chardonnay

2 cups heavy cream

2 cups sour cream

1 tablespoon minced fresh basil

Salt and freshly ground black pepper to taste

1 pound fettuccine, cooked in boiling salted water until al dente, then drained

For the roasted pepper purée: Preheat oven to 450°F. Lightly oil a baking sheet.

(recipe continued on next page)

Brush the bell peppers with the olive oil and place on the prepared baking sheet. Roast the peppers for about 30 minutes or until blackened. Remove from oven and place hot peppers in a plastic bag. Let them steam in the bag until cool. Peel off the skins and discard. Place the red bell peppers in a blender with the lemon juice and purée. Set aside.

In a large saucepan, melt the butter over medium heat. Add the onion and sauté until translucent. Add the wine and simmer until liquid has almost evaporated. Stir in the reserved bell pepper purée, cream, and sour cream. Simmer until mixture is reduced by half. Stir in basil and season with salt and pepper. Toss hot pasta with sauce and serve immediately.

Serves 6
Serve with Handley Cellars Dry Creek Chardonnay

IRON HORSE VINEYARDS

Ten miles from the Pacific coast and sixty-five miles north of San Francisco lie Iron Horse Vineyards, named for the railroad stop it once was. Barry and Audrey Sterling, along with their partner and Vineyard Manager, Forrest Tancer, have created a vineyard that is known as one of the premier wineries in the United States. In addition to their well-known and sought after sparkling wines, they produce outstanding still wines from their vineyards in Sonoma County's Green and Alexander Valleys.

The Sterlings and Forrest all live on their land and give daily care and attention to their vineyards, thus assuring consistency and high quality wines.

PENNE
with Chanterelles

The intense flavors of forest-harvested Chanterelles provides an excellent foil for the crisp and bold flavors of the Iron Horse Blanc de Blancs.

3 shallots, minced

1/2 cup Iron Horse Vineyards Blanc de Blancs

5 tablespoons butter

2 cups chanterelles, sliced

1 cup heavy cream

6 ounces Parmesan, freshly grated

1/4 cup sour cream

2 tablespoons minced fresh parsley

1 teaspoon salt

1/4 teaspoon white pepper

1 pound penne, cooked in boiling salted water until al dente, then drained

Chopped fresh parsley, for garnish

In a saucepan, combine shallots and wine. Simmer over medium heat until mixture is reduced to a syrup. Add butter and chanterelles and sauté until tender. Stir in cream and reduce by one-third. Stir in Parmesan, sour cream, parsley, salt, and pepper and cook until heated through.

Toss hot pasta with sauce and sprinkle with chopped parsley. Serve immediately.

Serves 6
Serve with Iron Horse Vineyards
Blanc de Blancs

I love everything that's old:
old friends, old times, old manners,
old books, old wine.

Oliver Goldsmith

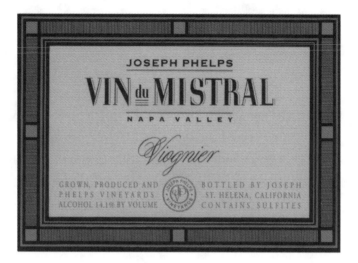

JOSEPH PHELPS VINEYARDS

Few wineries in Northern California have more "firsts" to their name than the winery of Joseph Phelps. "Insignia," the first Bordeaux-style blend to be produced in California as a proprietary wine, ushered in the era of the "Meritage" wines. His 1974 Syrah was perhaps the first time that variety had been bottled as such. And since 1990, his Vin du Mistral wines have epitomized the classic Rhone varietals.

Located in a stunning redwood building, the winery is anchored to the landscape by a massive wisteria-covered trellis made from 100-year-old recycled bridge timbers. It is definitely worth an appointment to visit this pioneer of the modern Napa Valley.

TURKEY SCALOPPINI
with a Banana-Pecan Crust over Farfalle with Sautéed Vegetables

Trey Blankenship devised the incredibly delicious combination of flavors for this signature dish.

1 pound boneless, skinless turkey breast

Salt and freshly ground black pepper to taste

2 bananas, mashed

1 teaspoon oregano

1 teaspoon sage

3/4 cup fresh plain breadcrumbs

3/4 cup pecans, lightly toasted and ground

1/4 cup olive oil

1 teaspoon rosemary

1 shallot, minced

1 clove garlic, minced

4 carrots, julienned

1 yellow summer squash, julienned

1 small red bell pepper, diced

1/2 cup Joseph Phelps Vineyards Chardonnay

1/4 cup butter, softened

1 tablespoon honey

8 ounces farfalle pasta (bowtie), cooked in boiling salted water until al dente, then drained

3 scallions, chopped

(recipe continued on next page)

🍂 Preheat oven to warm, 200°F.

Cut the turkey along the grain into 4 thin slices. Pound lightly with a meat mallet until 1/4-inch thick. Season turkey slices with salt and pepper. Set aside.

In a shallow dish, blend mashed bananas with oregano and sage until smooth. In a separate shallow dish, stir together breadcrumbs and pecans. Dredge turkey in banana mixture. Place turkey in breadcrumb mixture and pat to coat with mixture. In a large nonstick skillet, heat olive oil over medium-high heat. Carefully place turkey in hot oil and sear well on both sides. Transfer turkey to a baking sheet and keep warm in the oven.

Add the rosemary, shallot and garlic to the skillet and sauté until fragrant. Add the carrots, summer squash, red pepper, and wine. Reduce heat to medium-low and simmer until vegetables are tender and liquid has almost evaporated. Stir in butter and honey. Season with salt and pepper. Toss hot pasta with vegetables and divide onto 4 plates. Place a turkey breast scaloppini on the pasta and sprinkle with scallions. Serve immediately.

Serves 4
Serve with Joseph Phelps Vineyards
Chardonnay

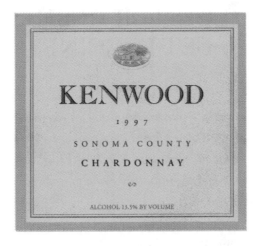

KENWOOD VINEYARDS AND WINERY

At Kenwood Vineyards and Winery each vineyard lot is handled separately within the winery to preserve its individuality. Such "small lot" winemaking allows the winemaker to bring each lot of wine to its fullest potential. This style of winemaking is evident in the quality of Kenwood Vineyards and Winery's special bottlings. From the Jack London Vineyard series, whose grapes come from the historical lava-terraced vineyards of the Jack London Ranch, to the Artist Series Cabernet Sauvignon, whose labels each year feature the work of a renowned artist, Kenwood Vineyards and Winery's show Sonoma County at its best.

CREAMY OYSTER MUSHROOM FETTUCCINE

Kenwood Vineyards and Winery's executive chef, Linda Kittler combined asparagus, leeks, and oyster mushrooms with Kenwood Vineyards and Winery Chardonnay and came up with this tasty summer dish.

24 asparagus spears

1/3 cup butter, divided

3 leeks, white and pale green parts only, chopped

1 pound oyster mushrooms, stems removed and sliced

1 tablespoon minced fresh tarragon

2 cups Kenwood Vineyards and Winery Sonoma County Chardonnay

2 cups chicken stock

1 cup heavy cream

Salt and freshly ground black pepper to taste

1 pound fettuccine, cooked in boiling salted water until al dente, then drained

Blanch asparagus in boiling salted water for 2 minutes, then drain and plunge into an ice bath to cool. Drain and pat dry. Slice half of the asparagus into 2-inch pieces. Reserve 12 asparagus spears for garnish.

In a large skillet, heat 3 tablespoons of the butter over medium heat. Add leeks and sauté until tender but not brown. Add remaining butter, mushrooms, and tarragon and sauté until tender. Add wine and simmer until mixture is reduced by half. Add chicken stock and simmer until mixture is reduced by half. Add cream and simmer until mixture is reduced by half. Season with salt and pepper. Add sliced asparagus and simmer until sauce is heated through. Divide pasta onto 6 plates and top with sauce. Place 2 asparagus spears on top.

Serves 6
Serve with Kenwood Vineyards and Winery
Sonoma County Chardonnay

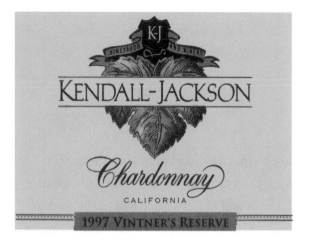

KENDALL-JACKSON WINERY

In 1974, Jess Jackson and his family purchased an 85-acre pear ranch near Lakeport, in Northern California. By 1982 the ranch was a vineyard, the barn was a tasting room, and the pasture was a winery. Meanwhile, the Jackson Family studied the premium vineyards that span California's cool coastal growing regions and discovered the wonderful spectrum of flavors produced by the same grape varietal grown in different locations. They asked themselves, "Why not use this exciting diversity? Why not blend the best grapes from the best vineyards to produce unique wines with layers of depth and complexity?"

Their first Chardonnay was made in 1982 from vineyards in Santa Barbara, Monterey, Sonoma, and Lake Counties. This wine was named "Best American Chardonnay" by the American Wine Competition. Their concept of blending the best with the best was affirmed and to this day continues to be the reason their wines are noted for their consistency and complexity, vintage after vintage.

SPAGHETTI
with Fresh Herbs
& Mozzarella

This beautiful and fresh-tasting first course is
from Patricia Caringella, caterer extraordinaire.

1 bunch fresh basil, chopped

1 teaspoon minced fresh marjoram

1 teaspoon minced fresh oregano

1 teaspoon minced fresh thyme

$1/2$ cup olive oil

2 tomatoes, chopped

8 ounces fresh mozzarella, diced

Salt and freshly ground black pepper to taste

10 ounces spaghetti, cooked in boiling salted water
until al dente, then drained

In a large serving bowl, combine basil, marjoram, oregano, thyme, and olive oil. Stir in tomatoes
and mozzarella. Season well with salt and pepper.
Toss the drained hot spaghetti with the herb mixture. Taste for seasoning and serve immediately.

Serves 4
Serve with Kendall-Jackson Winery
Chardonnay

LA CREMA

La Crema has focused its efforts on the viti-cultural areas both within the cool Carneros and Russian River appellations and in those yet "undiscovered" regions that lie just outside and alongside those two winegrow-ing areas. This influence of cool maritime climates, coupled with painstaking atten-tion given to each individual lot of wine, has helped develop La Crema into one of Sonoma County's leading wineries.

FETTUCCINE ALFREDO

This variation on the original incorporates pine nuts, which add a savory texture to the traditional Alfredo sauce.

1 cup freshly grated Parmesan cheese

1/2 cup butter, softened

1/2 cup heavy cream

1/2 cup olive oil

1/2 cup pine nuts, ground

4 cloves garlic, minced

1 teaspoon salt

1/2 teaspoon white pepper

1/2 cup chopped fresh parsley

1 pound fettuccine, cooked in boiling salted water until al dente, then drained

In a saucepan, combine Parmesan, butter, cream, olive oil, pine nuts, garlic, salt, and white pepper. Stir over medium-low heat for about 10 minutes, or until mixture is smooth and the cheese has melted. Stir in parsley. Gently toss hot pasta with the sauce and serve immediately.

Serves 6 to 8
Serve with La Crema
Chardonnay

LEDSON WINERY AND VINEYARDS

One of Northern California's newest wineries, Ledson is rapidly making a name for itself with its reserve Merlots, floral and fruity Rieslings, and intense Chardonnays. Located in Sonoma County's Valley of the Moon, Ledson is at home in a fantastic brick and mortar gothic-style mansion known affectionately as "The Castle." Two full-time chefs guarantee Ledson's commitment to the art and culture of pairing food and great wine.

CAJUN PASTA
with Vegetables

Philip Abbott, chef at Ledson, developed this mild and flavorful Cajun pasta to show off and complement their fine wine.

CAJUN SPICE MIX:

3 tablespoons paprika

1 tablespoon garlic powder

2 teaspoons onion powder

1 teaspoon basil

1 teaspoon cayenne

1 teaspoon dry mustard

1 teaspoon oregano

1 teaspoon freshly ground black pepper

1 teaspoon salt

1 teaspoon thyme

1/2 teaspoon cumin

2 tablespoons vegetable oil

1 red onion, sliced

1 red bell pepper, julienned

6 ounces mushrooms, sliced

1 tomato, chopped

(recipe continued on next page)   **69**

2 cloves garlic, minced

2 tablespoons Cajun Spice Mix

1/2 cup Ledson Winery and Vineyards Monterey
 Johannisberg Riesling

1 1/2 cups heavy cream

1/2 teaspoon freshly squeezed lemon juice

12 ounces fusilli pasta, cooked in boiling salted
 water until al dente, then drained

2 tablespoons olive oil

1/4 cup freshly grated Parmesan cheese

For the Cajun Spice Mix: In a bowl, stir together all ingredients with a fork until well blended. Keep in an airtight jar.

In a large skillet, heat vegetable oil over medium-high heat. Add red onion, bell pepper, mushrooms, tomato, and garlic and sauté until tender. Stir in the Cajun Spice Mix and sauté until fragrant. Stir in wine and simmer until liquid has almost evaporated. Stir in cream and lemon juice. Toss drained pasta with olive oil and add to skillet. Simmer, stirring constantly, until the sauce is reduced by half. Divide into 4 shallow bowls and sprinkle with Parmesan.

Serves 4
Serve with Ledson Winery & Vineyards
Monterey Johannisberg Riesling

CITRUS RISOTTO *with Grilled Scallops & Shrimp & a Honey-Thyme Sauce*

The delicate and complex flavors in this citrus risotto owe their origins to Guerry McComas, chef at Ledson.

HONEY-THYME SAUCE:

1 tablespoon olive oil

1/2 cup finely chopped onion

4 cloves garlic, minced

1 1/2 cups Ledson Winery and Vineyards Napa Valley Sauvignon Blanc

2 cups heavy cream

1 tablespoon honey

1 tablespoon minced fresh thyme

Salt and freshly ground black pepper to taste

CITRUS RISOTTO:

1/4 cup olive oil

1 cup finely chopped red onion

2 cups arborio rice

1 cup Ledson Winery and Vineyards Sauvignon Blanc

2 cups water

(recipe continued on next page)

1 cup half-and-half

3/4 cup freshly grated Parmesan cheese

Juice of 1 orange

Zest of 1 orange, finely minced

Zest of 1 lemon, finely minced

2 tablespoons snipped fresh chives

Salt and freshly ground black pepper to taste

12 scallops

12 ounces shelled medium shrimp

Salt and freshly ground black pepper to taste

2 tablespoons olive oil

For the sauce: In a saucepan, heat olive oil over medium heat. Add onion and garlic and sauté until translucent. Stir in wine and simmer until liquid is reduced to 1/4 cup. Stir in cream and simmer until liquid is reduced by half. Stir in honey and thyme and bring to a simmer. Season with salt and pepper. Pour sauce through a sieve and discard the solids. Set sauce aside and keep warm.

For the risotto: In a large saucepan, heat olive oil over medium heat. Add red onion and sauté until translucent. Stir in rice and sauté until it is just translucent around the edges. Stir in wine and simmer, stirring constantly, until liquid is almost absorbed. Stir in water and simmer, stirring constantly, until liquid is almost absorbed. Add half-and-half and simmer, stirring constantly, until liquid is only slightly absorbed. Stir in Parmesan, orange juice, orange zest, lemon zest, and chives. Continue stirring until texture is creamy and rice is tender but still firm.

Season scallops and shrimp with salt and pepper. In a skillet, heat olive oil over medium-high heat. Add scallops and shrimp and sauté until seared on both sides and just cooked through.

Divide risotto onto 6 plates and top with seafood. Spoon a little sauce over the risotto and serve immediately.

Serves 6
Serve with Ledson Winery and Vineyards
Napa Valley Sauvignon Blanc

CHARDONNAY
RUSSIAN RIVER VALLEY
VINTAGE 1996

MARK WEST ESTATE VINEYARD AND WINERY

Certified organic since 1990, Mark West Estate Vineyard and Winery is located where the cooling effects of the nearby Pacific Ocean and the fogs of San Pablo Bay provide ideal growing conditions for their fruit. Their 66 acres of Chardonnay, Pinot Noir, Gewürztraminer, and Merlot, whose original plantings date back to 1974, show restrained elegance and delicate, yet multilayered fruit. Ideal to show off the nuances of a subtly seasoned cuisine, the wines of Mark West Estate Vineyard and Winery are proof positive that wine enhances a fine meal.

CHINESE RAVIOLI
with Ginger Cream Sauce

Barbara Hom at Night Owl Catering created this luscious ravioli with a rich and flavorful sauce.

GINGER CREAM SAUCE:

4 cups heavy cream

2-inch piece of fresh ginger, peeled and sliced

Salt and white pepper to taste

CHINESE RAVIOLI:

1 tablespoon olive oil

1 cup finely chopped baby bok choy

2 cloves garlic, minced

1 cup fully-cooked ground Smithfield ham

1 cup ground chicken

1 egg, lightly beaten

Round wonton skins

For the ginger cream sauce: In a saucepan, combine cream and ginger. Simmer over medium-low heat until mixture is reduced by half. Season with salt and white pepper. Strain out ginger and discard. Keep sauce warm.

(recipe continued on next page)

For the Chinese ravioli: In a skillet, heat olive oil over medium heat. Add bok choy and garlic and sauté until tender. Set aside to cool.

In a large bowl, combine cooled bok choy mixture, ham, chicken, and egg and stir until well blended.

Place wonton skins on a work surface and brush lightly with water. Place a tablespoon of filling in the center. Fold over to make a half-moon shaped ravioli and seal the edges together. Lightly sprinkle a baking sheet with flour. Place ravioli on baking sheet so that they are not touching each other. Continue until all filling is used.

Bring a large pot of salted water to a boil. Add the ravioli and cook until they rise to the surface, about 4 minutes. Drain and divide ravioli onto 4 plates. Top with the ginger cream sauce.

Serves 4
Serve with Mark West Estate Vineyard and Winery Russian River Valley Chardonnay

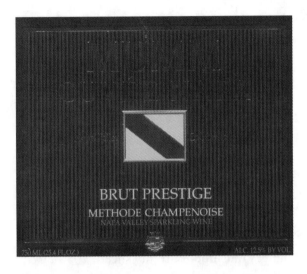

BRUT PRESTIGE
METHODE CHAMPENOISE
NAPA VALLEY SPARKLING WINE
750 ML (25.4 FL.OZ.)   ALC. 12.5% BY VOL.

MUMM CUVÉE NAPA

Journey through the vineyards, along the peaceful Silverado Trail and come for a visit. You'll see why we chose this glorious place for our home.

Imagine yourself on a terrace, seated under the cool shade of an elegant umbrella. The sun is setting over the Mayacamas mountains in the distance with soft amber and purple hues settling over the hills and vineyards. These images are reflected in your hand by a flute of America's finest sparkling wine—Mumm Cuvée Napa.

VEAL
with Champagne, Lemon, & Capers over Linguine

The classic flavors of Veal Piccata are enhanced by the addition of Mumm sparkling wine.

1/4 cup butter

1 pound veal scaloppini, julienned

Salt and freshly ground black pepper to taste

8 ounces mushrooms, thinly sliced

1 1/2 cups Mumm Cuvée Napa Brût Prestige

1/4 cup freshly squeezed lemon juice

3 tablespoons capers, rinsed

3 egg yolks

1 pound linguine, cooked in boiling salted water
    until al dente, then drained

1/4 cup chopped fresh Italian parsley

In a large skillet, melt the butter over medium heat. Season veal with salt and pepper, add to skillet, and sauté until lightly golden on all sides. Add the mushrooms and sauté until tender. Stir in the wine, lemon juice, and capers and simmer until the liquid is reduced by one-third. Reduce heat to medium-low.

Place egg yolks in a small bowl and whisk lightly. Pour about $1/4$ cup of the hot liquid in the skillet into the egg yolks and whisk to blend. Pour yolks back into the skillet and whisk to blend. Stir constantly until the sauce is thick enough to coat the back of a wooden spoon. Remove from heat and toss with the hot linguine until coated. Serve immediately in a large shallow bowl sprinkled with parsley.

Serves 6
Serve with Mumm Cuvée Napa
Brût Prestige

Drink no longer water,
but use a little wine
for thy stomach's sake.
The Bible

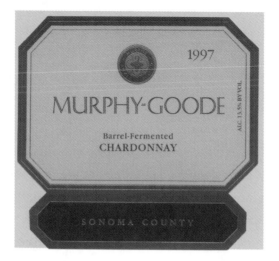

MURPHY-GOODE
WINERY

*Grape growers Tim Murphy and Dale Goode
teamed up with wine marketer Dave Ready in
1985 to form a family-owned winery in Sonoma
County's Alexander Valley. A lively and knowl-
edgeable trio, the partners combined creative vision,
hard work, and expertise to form their dynamic
wine estate. Murphy-Goode wines quickly earned a
reputation for consistently excellent, stylish wines.*

*Contemporary farming and incomparable grapes
are paramount to Murphy-Goode's success. Estate
vines grow on three Alexander Valley sites: Murphy-
Goode Vineyard, Murphy Ranch, and River
Ranch. Selected neighboring vineyards also provide
long-term grape sources to meet the continuing
demand for Murphy-Goode wines.*

BOWTIE PASTA
with Chicken, Mushrooms, & Artichokes

The talented Mary Lannin combined three classic ingredients to create this heartwarming main course.

SAUCE:

3 tablespoons olive oil

1 medium onion, finely chopped

3 cloves garlic, minced

2 cups sliced mushrooms

2 (8-ounce) cans tomato sauce

1 (14-ounce) can artichoke hearts, in brine, chopped

5 slices of prosciutto, julienned

2 teaspoons basil

2 teaspoons oregano

1/2 cup half-and-half

Salt and freshly ground black pepper to taste

4 skinless boneless chicken breasts

Salt and freshly ground black pepper to taste

12 ounces bowtie pasta, cooked in boiling salted water until al dente, then drained

Freshly grated Parmesan cheese

(recipe continued on next page)   *81*

For the sauce: In a large skillet, heat olive oil over medium heat. Add onion and garlic and sauté until translucent. Add mushrooms and sauté until mushrooms are lightly browned. Stir in tomato sauce, artichokes, prosciutto, basil, and oregano. Reduce heat to medium-low, cover, and simmer for 20 minutes. Stir in half-and-half, and season with salt and pepper to taste. Simmer uncovered until slightly thickened.

Prepare the grill. Season the chicken with salt and pepper. Grill over hot coals until cooked through. Divide the pasta onto 4 plates. Ladle sauce over and top with a grilled chicken breast. Sprinkle with Parmesan and serve immediately.

Serves 4
Serve with Murphy-Goode Winery
Chardonnay

QUAIL RIDGE CELLARS
AND VINEYARDS

Quail Ridge Cellars and Vineyards, Napa Valley's rustic gem, is nestled snugly in mid-Napa Valley. Quail Ridge's comfortable setting provides a welcome respite from the crowded surroundings of larger Napa wineries. Quail Ridge produces a number of excellent varietals that have won numerous medals in international wine competitions.

Located off Highway 29 on a 9-acre vineyard in the town of Rutherford, Quail Ridge Cellars and Vineyards is an integral part of the storied Rutherford Bench growing region. From its redwood deck, it is possible to enjoy the beauty and grandeur of the majestic Mayacamas mountain range, the historical divider of Napa and Sonoma Counties.

SHRIMP & SCALLOPS
with Spaghetti

Two delectable flavors of the sea, shrimp and scallops come together in this timeless recipe from Quail Ridge Cellars and Vineyards.

1/2 cup butter

1 tablespoon minced garlic

1 tablespoon minced shallots

1 cup sliced Portobello mushrooms

8 ounces medium shrimp

8 ounces scallops, halved

1/2 cup chicken stock

1/4 cup Quail Ridge Cellars and Vineyards Reserve
    Chardonnay

1/2 cup sliced red bell pepper

1/2 cup sliced scallions

Salt and freshly ground black pepper to taste

12 ounces spaghetti, cooked in boiling salted water
    until al dente, then drained

In a large skillet, heat butter over medium heat. Add garlic and shallots and sauté until fragrant. Add mushrooms and sauté until tender. Add shrimp and scallops and sauté until just cooked. Stir in chicken stock and wine and simmer until reduced by half. Add red bell pepper and scallions and simmer until just tender. Season with salt and pepper. Serve over hot pasta.

Serves 4
Serve with Quail Ridge Cellars and Vineyards
Reserve Chardonnay

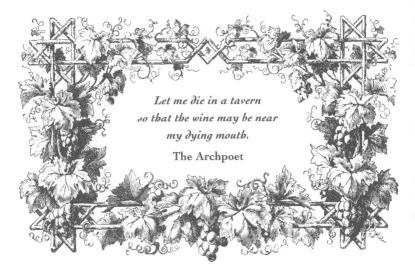

Let me die in a tavern
so that the wine may be near
my dying mouth.

The Archpoet

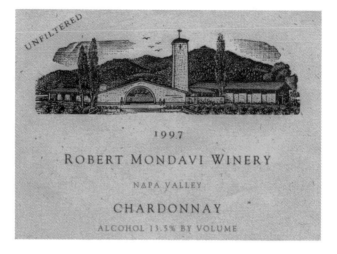

UNFILTERED

1997

ROBERT MONDAVI WINERY

NAPA VALLEY

CHARDONNAY

ALCOHOL 13.5% BY VOLUME

ROBERT MONDAVI WINERY

Founded in 1966 by Robert Mondavi and his son, Michael, the Robert Mondavi Winery is considered a leader in the modern wine industry. The Mondavis are committed to producing naturally balanced wines of great finesse and elegance that complement and enhance fine food. They have been successful in achieving these goals through Earth-friendly farming practices, a sophisticated winery emphasizing gentle treatment of their wines, and a genuine love for their handiwork. No other winery epitomizes the Napa Valley like the Robert Mondavi Winery.

RISOTTO
with Heirloom Tomatoes, Rock Shrimp, & Gremolata

If you haven't yet tasted garden fresh tomatoes, Robert Mondavi's executive chef Sarah Scott gives you reason enough to raise your own crop of tasty heirlooms.

GREMOLATA:

Zest of 2 lemons, finely minced

3 cloves garlic, minced

2 tablespoons minced fresh basil

2 tablespoons minced fresh mint

2 tablespoons minced Italian parsley

3 tablespoons olive oil

1 pound rock shrimp, diced

3 shallots, minced

2 1/2 cups arborio rice

1/2 cup Robert Mondavi Winery Chardonnay

7 cups chicken stock

2 pounds red and yellow heirloom tomatoes; peeled, seeded, and diced

1/4 cup butter

3 tablespoons freshly squeezed lemon juice

(recipe continued on next page)

For the gremolata: In a small bowl, stir together all ingredients, and set aside.

For the risotto: In a large pot, heat the olive oil over medium heat. Add the shrimp and sauté until just pink. Remove shrimp with a slotted spoon and set aside. Add shallots to the pot and sauté until tender. Stir in the rice and sauté until rice begins to turn light golden brown. Stir in the wine and simmer until the liquid has almost evaporated. In a saucepan, bring the chicken stock to a simmer over medium-low heat. Ladle enough simmering stock into the rice to just cover the rice. Lower the heat under the rice to medium-low and stir constantly until rice has almost absorbed all of the liquid. Add more simmering stock to just cover the rice and continue stirring until almost absorbed. Repeat this process until the rice is tender but still firm. This will take about 20 minutes. Stir in reserved shrimp, tomatoes, and butter. Stir in the gremolata and lemon juice. Serve immediately.

Serves 6
Serve with Robert Mondavi Winery
Chardonnay

SCHWEIGER VINEYARDS
AND WINERY

Fred and Sally Schweiger have turned their estate winery into one of the most picturesque properties in the Napa Valley. Located high above St. Helena atop Spring Mountain, their vines have found ideal growing conditions within the volcanic ash soils of this section of the Mayacamas mountain range.

Chardonnay, Merlot, and Cabernet Sauvignon are the three varieties upon which the Schweigers have built their reputation. Opulent with fruit, the red wines exhibit firm tannins and fine structure, while their Chardonnay astounds with supple mouth-filling elegance.

LINGUINE & MUSSELS
in Saffron Beurre Blanc

*Saffron lends an exotic and seductive aroma,
Chardonnay gives the broth that certain extra.
Have a loaf of extra crispy sourdough on hand
to enjoy every last drop.*

2 cups Schweiger Vineyards and Winery
    Chardonnay

2 shallots, minced

1 teaspoon saffron threads

1/2 teaspoon salt

1/4 cup heavy cream

1/2 cup cold butter, cut into small pieces

1 tablespoon minced fresh Italian parsley

48 mussels, scrubbed and debearded

8 cups water, divided

1 pound linguine

In a saucepan, whisk together wine, shallots, saffron, and salt. Bring to a simmer over medium heat and simmer until mixture is reduced to 1 cup. Whisk in cream and bring to a simmer. Remove saucepan from heat. Whisk in butter, one piece at a time, until all butter is incorporated. Stir in parsley and keep barely warm. Do not let simmer or sauce will separate.

In a large pot, combine mussels and 3 cups of water. Cover pot and bring to a boil over high heat. Steam for about 3 minutes until mussels open. With a slotted spoon, remove mussels and set aside. Discard any unopened mussels. Add remaining 5 cups of water to the pot and bring to a boil. Add the linguine and cook until al dente, then drain. Divide the pasta into 6 shallow bowls. Top each bowl with 8 mussels. Spoon a little sauce into the mussels and serve immediately.

Serves 6
Serve with Schweiger Vineyards and Winery Chardonnay

RODNEY STRONG
VINEYARDS

Over 35 years ago Rodney Strong was one of the first to recognize Sonoma County's potential for excellence. After searching for vineyard land that would bring each grape variety to its fullest potential, Rodney Strong finally selected vineyard sites in the Chalk Hill, Alexander Valley, and Russian River Valley appellations to produce his wine. In the cellar, he employs the subtle use of barrel and stainless steel fermentation, oak aging, and other winemaking techniques to bring out the best in the fruit. It is his philosophy to allow the grapes from each vineyard to express their individual character in the final bottled wine.

LEMON CREAM ORZO

This is a perfect side dish next to simply grilled sea bass or swordfish.

8 ounces Parmesan cheese, freshly grated

1 cup heavy cream

1/4 cup butter, softened

2 tablespoons olive oil

Juice of 1 lemon

Zest of 1 lemon, finely minced

1 teaspoon salt

1/4 teaspoon white pepper

2 tablespoons boiling water

1 pound orzo pasta

In a saucepan, stir together Parmesan, cream, butter, olive oil, lemon juice, lemon zest, salt, white pepper, and boiling water. Bring to a bare simmer over medium-low heat and stir for 5 minutes. Cook pasta in boiling, salted water until al dente. Drain well in a sieve. Gently stir pasta into the sauce until well coated. Serve immediately.

Serves 6 to 8
Serve with Rodney Strong Vineyards Chardonnay

SEAVEY VINEYARD

More than 120 years ago the vineyards the Seaveys now culti-vate were planted with grapes to make "claret of high repute," judged by the St. Helena Star *of that day to be "as fine as one might find anywhere." This was back when Conn Valley Road was little more than a wagon trail and the label of the wine was "Franco-Swiss Cellar" under the ownership of G. Crochat & Co. After the breakup of the company in the early 1900s, no more grapes were grown on the property until Bill and Mary Seavey acquired it and began to replant the vineyards in 1981, with Chardonnay in the cooler areas along Conn Creek, and Cabernet Sauvignon on the adjoining south-facing hillsides. In 1986, the Seaveys acquired land above their property and added small blocks of Merlot, Cabernet Franc, and Petite Verdot as well as more Cabernet Sauvignon for a current total of 38 acres of vineyard. In 1990 they completed renova-tion of the 1881 stone barn as their small winery, and began selecting grapes for limited lots of estate produced Cabernet Sauvignon and Chardonnay.*

MONTEREY BAY ABALONE
with Angel Hair Pasta

This dish is adapted from a recipe developed by Chef Jean Pierre Moulle at Chez Panisse Restaurant using farmed abalone from the Monterey Abalone Company.

$^1/_2$ cup finely diced sourdough bread

1 tablespoon butter, melted

4 tablespoons olive oil, divided

3 shallots, minced

2 cloves garlic, minced

8 ounces enoki mushrooms, sliced

$^1/_2$ cup Seavey Vineyard Chardonnay

Juice of 1 lemon

2 tablespoons butter, softened

1 tablespoon minced fresh chives

1 tablespoon minced fresh parsley

Salt and freshly ground black pepper to taste

12 ounces angel hair pasta, cooked in boiling salted water until al dente, then drained

1 pound abalone steaks, thoroughly pounded until tenderized and $^1/_8$-inch thick

(recipe continued on next page)

🍂 **For the breadcrumbs:** Preheat oven to 350°F. Lightly oil a baking sheet.

Place breadcrumbs on the prepared baking sheet. Toss the breadcrumbs with melted butter until evenly moistened. Bake for about 5 minutes, or until golden brown. Set aside.

In a skillet, heat 3 tablespoons of the olive oil over medium heat. Add shallots and garlic and sauté until fragrant. Add mushrooms and sauté until just tender. Stir in wine and lemon juice and simmer until mixture is reduced by half. Remove from heat and stir in softened butter, chives, parsley, salt, and pepper. Gently stir in hot pasta until well coated.

In a skillet, heat the remaining olive oil over medium-high heat. Season the abalone steaks with salt and pepper. When oil is hot, add the abalone and cook for about 1 minute per side. Do not over-cook or abalone will become tough. Divide pasta onto 4 plates and top with abalone. Sprinkle with breadcrumbs and serve immediately.

Serves 4
Serve with Seavey Vineyard
Chardonnay

SHAFER VINEYARDS

Located in the heart of the Stags Leap District of the Napa Valley, Shafer Vineyards has become synonymous with the finest the Napa Valley has to offer. Since their first crush in 1978, John Shafer and his son Doug have presided over the slow but steady growth of their premium winery from its first 1000-case production to its present size. Highly acclaimed by colleagues within the wine industry, the wines from Shafer Vineyards reflect their "terroir" *through their complex spectrum of aromas and flavors.*

LINGUINE
with Shrimp, Sundried Tomatoes, & Arugula

Barbara Shafer's recipe for her favorite pasta dish combines three intensely and wonderfully flavored ingredients for an unforgettable summer meal.

1 bunch arugula, chopped

1/4 cup chopped fresh basil

6 tablespoons olive oil, divided

1 1/2 tablespoons freshly squeezed lemon juice

3/4 cup sundried tomatoes (packed in oil and drained), thinly sliced

2 tablespoons minced garlic

1 pound medium shrimp, peeled and deveined

Salt and freshly ground black pepper to taste

12 ounces linguine, cooked in boiling salted water until al dente, then drained

4 sprigs basil for garnish

In a large bowl, combine arugula, basil, 1/4 cup olive oil, and lemon juice. Set aside.

In a skillet, heat remaining 2 tablespoons olive oil over medium heat. Add sundried tomatoes and garlic and sauté until fragrant. Add shrimp and sauté until cooked through. Add to arugula mixture and toss to mix. Season with salt and pepper. Add hot pasta to mixture and toss to coat well. Divide onto 4 plates and garnish with a sprig of basil. Serve immediately.

Serves 4
Serve with Shafer Vineyards
Red Shoulder Ranch Chardonnay

From wine
what sudden friendship springs!
John Gay

STERLING VINEYARDS

Built in the architectural style of the Greek Island of Mykonos, the Sterling Vineyards winery sits dramatically on top of a 300-foot knoll just south of Napa Valley's northernmost town, Calistoga. Its white, monastic buildings contrast sharply with the dark green of the trees that cover the knoll. Visitors are carried up to the winery by aerial tramway and treated to a spectacular view of the Napa Valley below, as well as a close-up look at the Napa Valley's most dramatic and recognizable winery. The panorama is awe-inspiring and peaceful, punctuated only by the peal of Sterling's antique English church bells.

ORZO *with Chicken, Porcini Mushrooms, & Pancetta*

The rice-sized grains of orzo blend so intimately with the porcini mushrooms and pancetta that each bite is a completely unforgettable experience.

1 cup dried porcini mushrooms

1 cup Sterling Vineyards Sauvignon Blanc

1/4 cup olive oil, divided

4 ounces pancetta, finely chopped

8 ounces skinless, boneless chicken thighs, cut into 1/4-inch cubes

8 ounces small button mushrooms, quartered

2 tablespoons butter

1 tablespoon minced garlic

1 tablespoon minced fresh thyme

1 cup chicken stock

1 pound orzo pasta, cooked in boiling salted water until al dente, then drained

4 ounces freshly grated Parmesan cheese, divided

In a bowl, combine dried porcini mushrooms and wine. Cover and let stand overnight.

Drain porcini mushrooms and reserve the liquid. Coarsely chop porcini mushrooms and set aside.

(recipe continued on next page)

In a large skillet, heat 1 tablespoon of the olive oil over medium heat. Add the pancetta and sauté until slightly crisp. Transfer to a bowl. Add 1 tablespoon of the olive oil to the skillet and add the chicken. Sauté until golden brown, then add the chicken to the pancetta. Add the remaining olive oil to the skillet and add the reserved porcini mushrooms and the button mushrooms. Sauté until tender, then add to chicken mixture. Add the butter to the skillet. When the butter starts to sizzle, add the garlic and thyme and sauté until fragrant. Pour in the reserved porcini soaking liquid and chicken stock. Return the chicken mixture to the skillet and bring to a simmer. Stir in the hot orzo and simmer until most of the liquid is absorbed. Stir in half of the Parmesan until melted. Pour pasta into a large shallow bowl and sprinkle with the remaining Parmesan. Serve immediately.

Serves 6
Serve with Sterling Vineyards
Sauvignon Blanc

STONE CREEK WINERY

Stone Creek Wine Tasting Room is located in Kenwood in the heart of Sonoma County. The tasting room was once known as the Los Guilicos School. This historical one-room schoolhouse was built in 1890 and was one of the first public schools in the Los Guilicos Valley. The "Old Blue Schoolhouse" has a colorful history and is now the home of Stone Creek Wines.

LINGUINE & CLAMS
in Sauvignon Blanc

*Marc Downie of Catering by Design has created
this divine recipe fusing crisp Sauvignon Blanc and
briny clams. Serve with crusty bread to sop up the
savory broth.*

1 bottle Stone Creek Winery Sauvignon Blanc

1 (6-ounce) can clams and their liquid

3 tablespoons butter

3 tablespoons minced fresh cilantro

1 tablespoon freshly squeezed lemon juice

2 teaspoons basil

2 teaspoons minced fresh parsley

2 teaspoons rosemary

4 cloves garlic, minced

4 pounds live steamer clams, scrubbed well

1 pound linguine, cooked in boiling salted water
    until almost cooked, then drained

In a large pot combine wine, canned clams and their liquid, butter, cilantro, lemon juice, basil, parsley, rosemary, and garlic and bring to a boil over high heat. Boil until liquid is reduced by one-third. Add live clams, cover pot, and steam for about 3 minutes until clams open. Discard any unopened clams. With a slotted spoon, remove clams in shells to a large bowl. Reduce heat to medium and add semi-cooked linguine. Simmer until linguine is cooked through and broth is slightly reduced. Divide into 6 bowls and top with clams.

Serves 6
Serve with Stone Creek Winery
Sauvignon Blanc

SHELLS *Stuffed with Four Cheeses & Spinach Topped with Marinara Sauce & Béchamel*

This creation of Marc Downie will be the piéce de résistance *at your next informal dinner party.*

MARINARA SAUCE:

1 (28-ounce) can crushed tomatoes

1$^{1}/_{2}$ cups water

1 tablespoon tomato paste

4 cloves garlic, minced

1 tablespoon basil

1 tablespoon oregano

1 tablespoon thyme

$^{1}/_{2}$ cup chopped onion

2 carrots, chopped

2 ribs celery, chopped

Salt and freshly ground black pepper to taste

BÉCHAMEL SAUCE:

1 1/4 cups milk

3 whole cloves

1/4 teaspoon white pepper

1/8 teaspoon nutmeg

2 tablespoons butter, softened

2 tablespoons all-purpose flour

SHELLS STUFFED
WITH FOUR CHEESES:

1 (15-ounce) container ricotta cheese

6 ounces Monterey jack cheese, grated

6 ounces mozzarella cheese, grated

2 ounces Parmesan cheese, grated

1 (10-ounce) box frozen chopped spinach, thawed
and squeezed as dry as possible

1 egg, lightly beaten

Salt and freshly ground black pepper to taste

1 (12-ounce) package large pasta shells

🍇 Preheat oven to 350°F. Lightly oil a 13 x 9-inch baking dish.

For the marinara sauce: In a large saucepan, stir together tomatoes, water, tomato paste, garlic, basil, oregano, and thyme. In the bowl of a food processor, combine onion, carrots, and celery and process until finely minced. Add to tomato mixture and bring to boil. Reduce heat to medium-low and simmer until sauce is reduced by one-fourth. Season with salt and pepper and set aside.

For the béchamel sauce: In a saucepan, simmer the milk, cloves, white pepper, and nutmeg over low heat for 5 minutes. Remove the cloves and discard. In a separate saucepan, whisk together the butter and flour until it forms a smooth paste. Cook butter mixture over medium heat until it is bubbly. Slowly whisk in milk until smooth. Simmer over medium-high heat, whisking constantly, until slightly thickened. Remove from heat and set aside.

For the stuffed shells: In a large bowl, stir together ricotta, Monterey jack, mozzarella, Parmesan, spinach, and egg until well blended. Season with salt and pepper. Cook the pasta shells according to the directions on the package, until they are

slightly undercooked; they will finish cooking in the oven. Drain the shells thoroughly. Stuff each shell with 1 tablespoon of the filling. Place stuffed shells in a single layer in the prepared baking dish. Pour marinara sauce evenly over the shells. Top with béchamel sauce. Bake for 30 to 35 minutes, or until bubbly and lightly browned on top.

Serves 6 to 8
Serve with Stone Creek Winery
Sierra Foothills Viognier

It is better to hide ignorance,
but it is hard to do
when we relax over wine

Heraclitus

M. TRINCHERO®

FOUNDER'S ESTATE

chardonnay

1997 NAPA VALLEY

ALC 13.5% BY VOL

SUTTER HOME
WINERY

The Trinchero family, owners of Sutter Home Winery in the Napa Valley, created the ultra-premium M. Trinchero brand to honor the memory of their father, Mario, who purchased Sutter Home Winery in 1947 and worked tirelessly to make it a success. M. Trinchero Founder's Estate wines are produced exclusively from Napa Valley grapes by acclaimed winemaker Derek Holstein in a state-of-the-art facility carved out of the larger Sutter Home Winery. They are vinified using traditional French techniques and aged in the finest French and American barrels.

FETTUCCINE
with Halibut Medallions
& Lobster Vinaigrette

One of the Napa Valley's leading wineries is also home to one of the Valley's leading chefs. Jeffrey Starr, chef at Sutter Home, created this most voluptuous and seductive entrée. This is what you can do when you've already made something using a whole lobster and don't know what to do with the head and shell.

LOBSTER VINAIGRETTE:

Head and shell of 1 lobster

3 cups water

1/4 cup champagne vinegar

2 tablespoons chopped Italian parsley

1 tablespoon minced shallot

1 tablespoon Dijon mustard

1 teaspoon sugar

Salt and freshly ground black pepper to taste

1/2 cup olive oil

8 ounces pearl onions, peeled

2 tablespoons sugar

2 cups salted water

8 ounces English peas, shelled

(recipe continued on next page)

^{1}/4 cup olive oil, divided

8 ounces shiitake mushrooms, thinly sliced

2 tablespoons butter

1 pound baby spinach

4 (6-ounce) halibut fillets, each cut into 3 pieces

Salt and freshly ground black pepper to taste

1 pound fettuccine, cooked in boiling salted water
until al dente, then drained

^{1}/2 cup diced tomatoes for garnish

For the lobster vinaigrette: Combine lobster head and shell and water in a saucepan and simmer over medium heat until liquid is reduced to ^{1}/2 cup. Strain through a fine sieve and discard the solids.

In a bowl, whisk together the lobster stock, vinegar, parsley, shallot, mustard, sugar, salt, and pepper. Slowly add the olive oil in a thin stream, whisking constantly. Set aside.

In a small saucepan, combine pearl onions, sugar, and just enough water to cover. Cook over medium-high heat for about 10 minutes, or until tender. Drain and transfer to a bowl.

In a saucepan, bring the 2 cups of salted water to a boil. Add the peas and boil for 3 minutes.

Drain, then plunge into ice water to refresh the peas. Drain again and transfer to the bowl with the pearl onions.

In a skillet, heat 2 tablespoons of the olive oil over medium heat. Add the mushrooms and sauté until tender. Transfer to the bowl with pearl onions and peas. Add 1 tablespoon of the lobster vinaigrette to the vegetable mixture to moisten. Set aside.

In a saucepan, heat the butter over medium heat. Add the spinach and sauté until wilted. Set aside.

Season the halibut medallions with salt and pepper. In a skillet, heat the remaining 2 tablespoons of olive oil over medium-high heat. Add the halibut and sear on both sides. Take care not to overcook, the halibut should be just cooked through but still moist.

To assemble, rewarm vegetable mixture and spinach separately. Divide hot pasta between 4 plates. Place spinach on top of fettuccine. Place 3 halibut medallions on the spinach and divide vegetable mixture over the halibut. Stir the vinaigrette and spoon over the vegetables. Sprinkle with chopped tomatoes and serve immediately.

Serves 4
Serve with M. Trinchero
Chardonnay

TURNBULL WINE CELLARS

Located just south of world-renowned Oakville in the Napa Valley, Patrick O'Dell, proprietor of Turnbull Wine Cellars, produces stunning wines of amazing complexity and depth. His well known red wines include Cabernet Sauvignon, Merlot, and Sangiovese, as well as small amounts of Syrah and Zinfandel. A limited amount of elegant Sauvignon Blanc is a special treat for white wine lovers who visit his tasting room.

ORECCHIETTE
with Smoked Salmon
& Sauvignon Blanc

The incomparable Beverley Wolfe, Turnbull's genius de la cuisine, marries the sublime flavors of smoked salmon with their crisp Sauvignon Blanc in this unforgettable recipe.

2 cups heavy cream

15 parsley stems, tied in a bundle with kitchen string

2 tablespoons olive oil

1 tablespoon finely minced lemon zest

3 cloves garlic, minced

1/2 cup Turnbull Wine Cellars Sauvignon Blanc

2 cups fresh or frozen peas

6 ounces smoked salmon, chopped

Salt and freshly ground black pepper to taste

12 ounces orecchiette pasta, cooked in boiling salted water until al dente, then drained

4 teaspoons black caviar for garnish

Chopped parsley for garnish

(recipe continued on next page)

In a saucepan, simmer cream and parsley stems over medium-low heat until cream is reduced by half. Discard parsley and set cream aside.

In a large skillet, heat olive oil over medium heat. Add lemon zest and garlic and sauté until fragrant. Stir in wine and simmer until liquid is reduced by half. Stir in reserved cream, peas, and smoked salmon and season with salt and pepper. Bring to a simmer and gently stir in hot pasta until well coated. Divide onto 4 plates. Sprinkle with caviar and chopped parsley and serve immediately.

Serves 4
Serve with Turnbull Wine Cellars
Sauvignon Blanc

I drank at every vine.
The last was like the first.
I came upon no wine
As wonderful as thirst.

Millay

V. SATTUI WINERY

V. Sattui Winery is a family-owned winery established in 1885, and located in St. Helena, the very heart of California's famous Napa Valley. Their award-winning wines are sold exclusively at the winery, by mail order, and from their website direct to customers. Surrounding the beautiful stone winery is a large tree-shaded picnic ground. V. Sattui also boasts a large gourmet cheese shop and deli.

CICERI & TRIA
(Chickpeas and Pasta)

*This unusual combination of soft and crisp
pasta, from Robert O'Malley, is a specialty of
the Puglia region in Southern Italy.*

1 onion, chopped

1 carrot, chopped

1 rib celery, chopped

2 cloves garlic

1/4 cup lightly packed fresh Italian parsley leaves

8 ounces Roma tomatoes, chopped

1 bay leaf

Boiling water

2 (15-ounce) cans chickpeas

Salt and freshly ground black pepper to taste

10 ounces dry tagliatelle, divided in half

1/4 cup olive oil

In the bowl of a food processor, combine onion,
carrot, celery, garlic, and parsley and pulse until
finely chopped. Transfer mixture to a large saucepan and add tomatoes and bay leaf. Add just
enough boiling water to barely cover the vegetables.

Bring to a simmer over medium-low heat, cover and simmer for about 45 minutes. Stir in chickpeas and their liquid. Bring to a boil, then reduce heat to medium, and continue to simmer, uncovered, for an additional 30 minutes, or until sauce has slightly thickened. Stir often to keep sauce from scorching. Season with salt and pepper and keep warm.

Bring a large pot of salted water to a boil. Add half of the pasta and cook until al dente. Drain and place in a large serving bowl. Add the sauce and stir gently until coated. Keep warm.

Break the remaining dry tagliatelle into small pieces. Heat the olive oil in a skillet over medium-high heat. When the oil is hot, add the dry pasta and stir with a wooden spoon. Continue stirring for 1 or 2 minutes, or until the pasta begins to slightly swell up, crisp, and turn a light golden brown. Immediately add the fried pasta and olive oil to the serving bowl and stir gently until well mixed. Serve immediately.

Serves 4
Serve with V. Sattui Winery
Chardonnay

THE WINERIES:

Arrowood Vineyards & Winery
14347 Sonoma Highway
Glen Ellen, CA 95442
707.938.5170

Beaulieu Vineyard
1960 St. Helena Highway
Rutherford, CA 94573
707.963.2411

Belvedere Vineyards and Winery
435 West Dry Creek Road
Healdsburg, CA 95448
707.433.8236

Benziger Family Winery
1883 London Ranch Road
Glen Ellen, CA 95442
707.935.3000

Beringer Vineyards
2000 Main Street
St. Helena, CA 94574
707.963.7115

Cakebread Cellars
8300 St. Helena Highway
Rutherford, CA 94573
707.963.5221

Canyon Road Winery
19550 Geyserville Avenue
Geyserville, CA 95441
707.857.3417

Cardinale Winery
Post Office Box 328
Oakville, CA 94562
707.944.2807

Cedar Mountain Winery
7000 Tesla Road
Livermore, CA 94550
510.373.6694

Chateau Montelena Winery
1429 Tubbs Lane
Calistoga, CA 94515
707.942.5105

De Loach Vineyards
1791 Olivet Road
Santa Rosa, CA 95401
707.526.9111

Dry Creek Vineyard
3770 Lambert Bridge Road
Healdsburg, CA 95448
707.433.1000

Ferrari-Carano Vineyards and Winery
8761 Dry Creek Road
Healdsburg, CA 95448
707.433.6700

Geyser Peak Winery
22281 Chianti Road
Geyserville, CA 95441
707.857.9463

Glen Ellen Winery
14301 Arnold Drive
Glen Ellen, CA 95442
707.939.6277

Gloria Ferrer Champagne Caves
23555 Highway 121
Sonoma, CA 95476
707.996.7256

Grgich Hills Cellar
1829 St. Helena Highway
Rutherford, CA 94573
707.963.2784

Handley Cellars
3153 Highway 128
Philo, CA 95466
707.895.3876

Iron Horse Vineyard
9786 Ross Station Road
Sebastopol, CA 95472
707.887.1337

Joseph Phelps Vineyards
200 Taplin Road
St. Helena, CA 94574
707.963.2745

Kendall-Jackson Winery
5007 Fulton Road
Santa Rosa, CA 95439
707.571.8100

Kenwood Vineyards and Winery
9592 Sonoma Highway
Kenwood, CA 95452
707.833.5891

La Crema
3690 Laughlin Road
Windsor, CA 95492
707.571.1504

Ledson Winery and Vineyards
7335 Sonoma Highway
Kenwood, CA 95452
707.833.2330

Mark West Estate Vineyard
    and Winery
7010 Trenton-Healdsburg Road
Forestville, CA 95436
707.544.4813

Mumm Cuvée Napa
8445 Silverado Trail
Rutherford, CA 94573
707.942.3434

Murphy-Goode Winery
4001 Highway 128
Geyserville, CA 95441
707.431.7644

Quail Ridge Cellars and Vineyards
1155 Mee Lane
Rutherford, CA 94573
707.963.9783

Robert Mondavi Winery
7801 St. Helena Highway
Oakville, CA 94562
707.226.1395

Rodney Strong Vineyards
11455 Old Redwood Highway
Healdsburg, CA 95448
707.433.6521

Schweiger Vineyards and Winery
4015 Spring Mountain Road
St. Helena, CA 94574
707.963.4882

Seavey Vineyard
1310 Conn Valley Road
St. Helena, CA 94574
707.963.8339

Shafer Vineyards
6154 Silverado Trail
Napa, CA 94558
707.944.9454

Sterling Vineyards
1111 Dunaweal Lane
Calistoga, CA 94515
707.942.3300

Stone Creek Winery
9380 Sonoma Highway
Kenwood, CA 95452
707.833.4455

Sutter Home Winery
100 St. Helena Highway, South
St. Helena, CA 94574
707.963.3104

Turnbull Wine Cellars
8210 St. Helena Highway
Oakville, CA 94562
800.887.6285

V. Sattui Winery
1111 White Lane
St. Helena, CA 94574
707.963.7774

THE CATERERS:

Catering by Design
Post Office Box 1866
Glen Ellen, CA 95442
707.935.0390

Night Owl Catering
Post Office Box 226
Sebastapol, CA 95472
707.823.1850

Monterey Abalone Company
160 Wharf #2
Monterey, CA 93940
831.646.0350

Patricia Caringella Catering
3418 South Shore Road
Lake Oswego, OR 97034
503.636.2952

Conversions

LIQUID

1 tablespoon = 15 milliliters

$1/2$ cup = 4 fluid ounces = 125 milliliters

1 cup = 8 fluid ounces = 250 milliliters

DRY

$1/4$ cup = 4 tablespoons = 2 ounces = 60 grams

1 cup = $1/2$ pound = 8 ounces = 250 grams

FLOUR

$1/2$ cup = 60 grams

1 cup = 4 ounces = 125 grams

TEMPERATURE

400 degrees F = 200 degrees C = gas mark 6

375 degrees F = 190 degrees C = gas mark 5

350 degrees F = 175 degrees C = gas mark 4

MISCELLANEOUS

2 tablespoons butter = 1 ounce = 30 grams